HIP-HOP hitmakers

THE STORY OF
CASH MONEY
RECORDS

terri dougherty

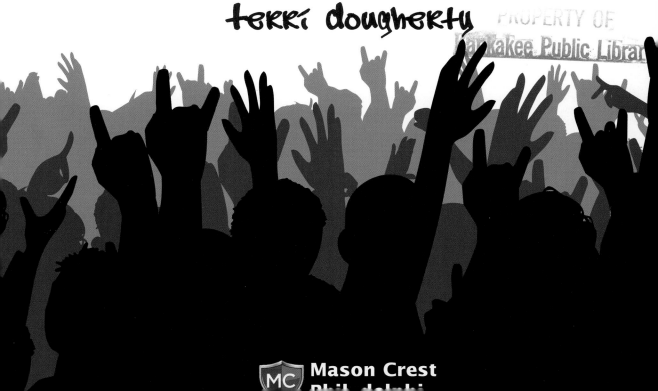

MC Mason Crest
Philadelphia

Mason Crest
370 Reed Road
Broomall, PA 19008
www.masoncrest.com

CPSIA Compliance Information: Batch #HHH040112-3.
For further information, contact Mason Crest at 1-866-MCP-Book

First printing
1 3 5 7 9 8 6 4 2

Library of Congress Cataloging-in-Publication Data

Dougherty, Terri.
  The story of Cash Money Records / Terri Dougherty.
    p. cm. — (Hip-hop hitmakers)
  Includes bibliographical references and index.
  ISBN 978-1-4222-2112-9 (hc)
  ISBN 978-1-4222-2125-9 (pb)
  ISBN 978-1-4222-9464-2 (ebook)
  1. Cash Money Records Inc.—History. 2. Record labels. I. Title.
  ML3792.C42D68 2012
  338.7'61782421649—dc23
                                              2011

3 1558 00276 9784

Photo credits: FilmMagic: 14; Getty Images: 24, 32, 34, 43, 46, 52; used under license from Shutterstock, Inc.: 12, 26, 37, 39; Helga Esteb / Shutterstock.com: 21, 48, 50, 51; DFree / Shutterstock.com: 4, 40; Marquis / Shutterstock.com: 44; Derrick Salters / Shutterstock.com: 33; Tristan Scholze / Shutterstock.com: 16; Noam Wind / Shutterstock.com: 7; Wikimedia Commons: 54; WireImage: cover, 8, 22.

Contents

Cash Money Records artists Lil Wayne and Nicki Minaj arrive at the 2011 Grammy Awards ceremony in Los Angeles. The success of Lil Wayne's album Tha Carter III helped make Cash Money Records a major player in the hip-hop world.

the Rise of the South

Fans did whatever they could to get a glimpse of Lil Wayne. They climbed over fences. They scrambled onto the roof. They knew he would be rapping "Lollipop," "A Milli," and other hits from his incredibly popular album *Tha Carter III* at the House of Blues in Los Angeles. Energy and excitement would roll through the club when he strutted onstage, and they wanted to be part of it.

The croaky voice of Lil Wayne was creating a frenzy with a summertime club appearance that was of part of a stellar year for the *rapper*. *Tha Carter III* sold 1 million copies in a single week. "Lollipop" topped Billboard's chart of the top 100 songs. Fans found his tracks online and packed arenas to see his live performances. Lil Wayne was the biggest rapper of the year in 2008, and the hard working entertainer showed no signs of slowing down. His rise to the top was even more impressive when fans considered where he came from.

ROOTED IN NEW ORLEANS

Lil Wayne is a native of New Orleans. He is the biggest star of Cash Money Records. Lil Wayne grew up in the city's 17th Ward, in a poor, tough neighborhood. Drugs, guns and crime were part of his environment. He faced temptations and challenges every day, but also found inspiration for his raps there.

=== FAST FACT ===

Lil Wayne's real name is Dwayne Michael Carter Jr.

As difficult as his surroundings were, they were not the only challenge Lil Wayne faced as he made his way to the top of the charts. He grew up in a city more famous for its jazz music than its rappers. In the mid-1990s, Wayne was a young teen and just getting started with his rap career at Cash Money. At that time, rap music was focused on the East and West coasts. Record companies such as Bad Boy Records in New York City and Death Row Records in Los Angeles dominated the music that was released. Southern-based Cash Money was a rap music outsider. Respect and recognition were slow to come its way.

BOUNCING TO THE BEAT

While Southern rap music was not well-known nationwide in the 1980s and '90s, it had a strong regional following. It was based on a style of music called *bounce*. Bounce's energetic rhymes were chanted

‍

BOUNCE EVOLVES

Bounce music began appearing at block parties in New Orleans in the 1980s. Most early bounce was built on an extended **sample** of music from the 1985 song "Drag Rap" by the Showboys, which also became known by the name "Triggerman."

The beat of bounce music also reflects the rhythms of second-line parades that are part of New Orleans' music history. These parades include a brass band and people dancing in the street, often with umbrellas and handkerchiefs. They are called second line parades because they follow the main line that is sponsoring the parade.

As the popularity of live bounce music performances grew, local producers began to record and sell the songs. The first bounce song to be recorded and sold was "Where Dey At" by New Orleans MC T.T. Tucker and producer DJ Irv. It was released in 1991 and sold on cassette to a local audience. Other early bounce recordings include "It's Jimi" by DJ Jimi, and "Do the Jubilee" by DJ Jubilee, which was released in 1995.

Bounce music draws on the sound of New Orleans bands.

Cash Money Records founders Bryan "Baby" Williams (left) and Ronald "Slim" Williams attend a 2011 event in New York City.

in call-and-answer style. The artists would deliver a rhyme and invite the audience to respond with a one or two-line refrain.

Audiences responded to bounce music's strong baseline and danceable beat. Some bounce songs included an element of local pride, with shout-outs to neighborhoods in New Orleans where the music had emerged. "Everybody was scared to talk about wards and projects in New Orleans," said bounce musician Gregory D. "Not me. I wanted to put the city on the map and represent New Orleans."

Bounce music lyrics emphasized bragging, arrogance and sexual prowess, and the music was also controversial. The explicit sexual nature of the lyrics offended some listeners. Some bounce songs were banned from school dances.

However, a number of local producers found an audience for bounce recordings. One of these was Cash Money Records. Founded by Bryan "Baby" Williams and Ronald "Slim" Williams, the label began recording local artists.

SURPRISING SUCCESS

The early years were rough ones for the *record label*. Baby and Slim would sell the cassettes out of their car. They had some local success, but bounce music was not well known outside of New Orleans. It took years for them to establish a national presence.

Before Lil Wayne was well known, artists such as B.G. (Baby Gangsta) and Juvenile (Terius Gray) helped Cash Money gain a foothold in the industry. Things looked bright for the company in the late 1990s, as a deal with a major record *distributor* boasted sales of 9 million albums. The label hit some tough times in the years that followed, however, as some of its most popular artists left the label. And even when Cash Money was able to sell a significant number of albums, awards and recognition from the music industry were slow to appear. Respect was difficult for the southern-based label to come by.

Things changed when Lil Wayne's popularity took off. Cash Money's status received a huge boost. Performers such as Drake, Kevin Rudolf, Jay Sean, and Nicki Minaj have further fueled Cash Money's success. These artists offered a broad base of musical styles, from rock to *rhythm and blues* and pop. Along with the unique and successful rap style of Lil Wayne, they give Cash Money Records the ability to appeal to varied musical tastes.

> **=== FAST FACT ===**
>
> New Orleans is divided into 17 wards. Residents often describe where they live with their ward number. Lil Wayne grew up in the Hollygrove neighborhood in the 17th Ward.

Cash Money endured its share of difficult times, from its beginnings in New Orleans to the loss of some of its early stars. However, Baby and Slim Williams have a knack for finding hard working artists who are dedicated to making music. Record labels rise, fall and self-destruct, but Cash Money has hung on thanks to its ability to catch rising stars and produce music that grabs listeners.

dollars for cash money

ash Money Records was founded by two brothers who grew up in Third Ward of New Orleans. Ronald "Slim" Williams and his brother Bryan "Baby" Williams lived in a rough neighborhood, where violence and drugs were part of life. Slim was nine and Baby was seven when their mother died. Their father remarried and they lived in a small house in the projects.

Their father, Johnny, ran a grocery store and bar. He worked a great deal, and although he did not have a lot of time to spend with his sons they learned about business from him. Since their father was often at work, that's where the boys went to be with him. "I used to go and work with my dad, help clean up, and he showed me how he ran

The historic St. Louis Cathedral is a well-known landmark in New Orleans. The statue in front represents Andrew Jackson, who won an important battle for the city during the War of 1812, and later served as the seventh president of the United States.

his little business," Slim said. "He wanted us to be our own entrepreneurs. So I learned to handle the money, the books."

In the early 1990s, Slim and Baby saw their opportunity to go into business for themselves. The local music scene had artists who could sell 10,000 CDs in the area, more than national artists sold there. Their father supported their idea and loaned them the money they needed to start Cash Money records.

Slim and Baby founded their record label in 1991, when Slim was 24 and Baby was 22. The first artist they signed was Kilo-G. His album, *Sleepwalker*, came out in 1992. Slim and Baby did not have a distributor to help them sell the recording, so they sold copies out of their car.

Cash Money began working with other artists who were part of the bounce music scene. Pimp Daddy, U.N.L.V, Ms. Tee, Lil' Slim, and Mr. Ivan helped them build a local following. They also worked with young rappers, who looked on Baby and Slim as father figures. One of their most promising rappers, B.G. (Christopher Dorsey), was only 11 when he started working with Cash Money. A few years later, Lil Wayne also joined Cash Money at age 11.

MANNIE FRESH WITH THE BEATS

A significant addition to the Cash Money label was producer Mannie Fresh (Byron Thomas). Not long after the brothers founded Cash Money, Fresh began mixing beats for its artists. Fresh's father was a DJ, and he learned how to create beats with a drum machine at a young age. He became a DJ himself and used keyboards and *synthesizers* to build on the rhythm. A talented producer, Fresh could quickly build a track for a rapper to work with.

Mannie Fresh (real name Byron Thomas) was the in-house music producer for Cash Money Records from 1993 until 2005. He helped to develop the label's distinctive sound.

While Fresh created the beats for Cash Label's bounce artists, he was not a fan of pure bounce music. He could not understand building every song off of one beat. "To me, it was the silliest thing in the world," he said. "It was basic, basic, basic. In the beginning, it was just chants." With a drum machine, synthesizer, and keyboard as his instruments, Fresh brought own style and creativity to bounce. He gave it an electro-hop under-current and began to produce Cash Money's signature sound.

CASH MONEY STARTS OVER

Cash Money's artists had some local success, with albums such as *6th and Baronne* (1993), and *Straight out Tha Gutta* (1994) by U.N.L.V. However, money was not rolling in. Slim and Baby and producer Mannie Fresh had one car to share. Fresh, who had a wife and daughter, brought in extra income by stealing cars.

The label had only been in business for a few years when Slim and Baby decided it was time to make a significant change. Slim and Baby were businessmen and saw that most of the Cash Money artists did not share the same attitude toward work as they did. The performers were not devoted to the business of music and their drug use also bothered the record label owners. "We was trying to teach them the way to do this thing—as far as handling meetings, signing autographs, doing interviews, showing up on time for shows—but they wasn't hungry enough," Slim said. "They'd make a little money and everything would just go to the wind. They were getting into drugs, smoking weed, and it was taking away from them handling their business. I was like, man, I can't deal with this, man. So I just woke up one morning and I told my brother, 'You know what, bruh, I got to get rid of everybody over here and start from scratch.'"

The music label cut ties with most of their performers in the mid-1990s. U.N.L.V., Kilo-G, Ms. Tee, and Lil' Slim were let go. However, the brothers continued to work with B.G., who was also known as Lil Doogie. He was not perfect, and Slim and Baby were aware of his troubles. As a teen, B.G. struggled with an addition to the drug heroin. His father had been killed when he was 12, and he began selling drugs make money. Despite this, Slim and Baby saw that he was a talented young rapper who had the right attitude and was someone they could work with. "B.G. had his problems," says Slim, "and he

> ## FAST FACT
> Three of Cash Money's early artists met violent deaths. Pimp Daddy (Edgar Givens) was killed in 1994 after an argument. Albert "Yella Boi" Thomas of UNLV died in 1997, and Kilo-g also died violently before Cash Money became a major record label.

was young, but he was hungry. You know, I learned that I'd rather deal with somebody that was about their business and was less talented than somebody that was talented and wasn't about their business. So

GANGSTA RAP

Gangsta rap was a controversial style of rap music that became popular in the late 1980s and early 1990s. One of the first gangsta rap albums was called *Straight Outta Compton*. It was released by N.W.A. in 1988 and included the song "Gangsta Gangsta," which celebrated hated and killing.

Crime and violence, including violence against women, were common themes in gangsta rap songs. Some said that gangsta rap reflected life on the streets of the inner city. Others, however, criticized gangsta rap for glorifying violence. The song "Cop Killer," written by Ice-T, was a troubling example. The lyrics talk about a person fed up with police brutality taking the law into his own hands and killing police officers. Negative reactions from police officers and political figures such as President George H.W. Bush caused Ice-T to pull the song from his *Body Count* album.

In 1996, rapper Dr. Dre said gangsta rap was dead. However, other rappers took the gangsta attitude and applied it to their own experiences. One of these was Cash Money artist B.G., who released gritty raps about drugs, death, and life on the streets of New Orleans.

The group N.W.A., featuring rapper Ice Cube, pioneered gangsta rap in the late 1980s.

we started working with him, showing him different styles, teaching him how to handle himself, and he was willing to learn."

Another artist that Cash Money began working with at this time was Lil Wayne. He was also a young rapper with a troubled life. He accidentally shot himself with a gun at his mother's home. However, Baby also saw him as another youngster he could take under his wing, and hoped to make a difference in his life.

Using the name the B.G.'s—which stands for Baby Gangstas—B.G. and Lil Wayne made their first album for Cash Money in the mid-1990s. On *True Story*, they rapped about growing up in poverty in the tough neighborhoods of New Orleans with tracks such as "From Tha 13th to Tha 17th" and "Hood Took Me Under."

NEW SOUND

True Story was the beginning of a new direction for Cash Money as began to move away from the bounce music that had given the label its start. Fresh saw that B.G. was a different kind of rapper than the other artists he had been working with at the label. Rather than pure bounce music, he gave B.G.'s songs more of a gangster sound.

B.G released his first solo album in 1996, *Chopper City*. The album moved more in the direction of hard-core **gangsta rap**. Fresh, who produced the album, blended synthesizer and guitar sounds. B.G. got personal with some of his songs. He rapped about the death of his father and his involvement with the wrong crowd in "So Much Death":

> *All he wanted me to do, be cool, stay in school*
> *But the dudes I hang with rearranged the whole attitude*
> *When he died, I started hustling to get paid*
> *I did the opposite, I know you turning in your grave."*

Moving away from pure bounce was a risky move for the label. It had a strong following in New Orleans, and the label was taking a chance that bounce fans would accept this new style. Their risk paid off, however, as Cash Money's new take on bounce music gave it a different edge that listeners approved of. "When it hit the street, it was like the new craze," Fresh said. "It left all the other cats that was doing bounce, like, five years behind."

Cash Money worked quickly to release more of this music. With help from Lil Wayne on some of the tracks, B.G. released *It's All On U, Vol. 1* and *It's All on U, Vol. 2*, the next year. The albums were a local success, selling more than 250,000 copies.

B.G. and Lil Wayne were not the only artists producing music for Cash Money. Juvenile, whose song "Bounce for the Juvenile" was a local hit in the early 1990s for another music label, released *Solja Rags* for Cash Money in 1997. The album sold 200,000 copies and was ranked on the Billboard R&B/Hip-Hop Albums chart, making it to number 55 nationwide. Like B.G., Juvenile's raps were influenced by his life in the Magnolia projects in New

> **FAST FACT**
>
> Juvenile's "Bounce for the Juvenile" appeared on DJ Jimi's album *It's Jimi.*

Orleans, which were also known as the C.J. Peete public-housing development. "My people played a big part in my career," he said. "I learned words, how to use words, how to talk slang—I got that from back there."

HOT BOYS

The young rappers who worked with Cash Money did not produce only solo efforts. They made frequent appearances on each others' albums. Lil Wayne, B.G. and other local rappers such as Magnolia Shorty, Turk, and Big Moe all contributed to the tracks on *Solja Rags*. Mannie Fresh also rapped on a few tracks. Baby and Mannie, who called themselves the Big Tymers, were part of B.G.'s albums, as were Lil Wayne, Turk, and Juvenile.

The most successful collaboration among Cash Money rappers was the creation of a group called the Hot Boys. B.G.,

> **FAST FACT**
>
> Cash Money Records founders Slim and Baby Williams are brothers but look and act very differently. Slim is tall and calm. Baby is robust and outgoing.

Juvenile, Turk, and Lil Wayne made up the group and released *Get It How U Live!* in 1997. It sold more than 400,000 copies and made it to No. 37 on the Billboard Top R&B/Hip Hop Albums chart.

Growing album sales were proof of the increasing popularity of the Cash Money artists. Baby was frustrated, however. The company still had only a regional reach. Riding on the success of *Solja Rags* and *Get It How U Live!*, he looked to expand beyond the South. To do this he began looking for a national record company that could make this happen.

3

Cash Money goes national

In the mid-1990s, national record distributors were beginning to notice the success that regional Southern music labels were having. Percy "Master P" Miller of No Limit Records, another Louisiana record label, got a distribution deal with Priority Records in 1995. With backing from Priority, he was able to reach a larger audience and became the first southern music hip hop producer to have national success. In 1998, No Limit Records sold 26 million albums.

The success of No Limit showed Baby that the best way for Cash Money to grow would be to enter into a deal with a national record distributor. Juvenile and Mannie Fresh were hesitant to get involved with a larger company, but Baby and Slim saw this as the best way for

The Williams brothers saw how Percy "Master P." Miller negotiated a distribution deal with a large national record company. They decided to do the same with Cash Money, making a deal with Universal Music.

Cash Money to reap more profits. In 1998, they negotiated a deal with Universal worth $30 million. The national company would help Cash Money with distribution and marketing, and Cash Money's artists would stay independent.

GROUP EFFORT

From the start, the albums that Cash Money's artists produced under the deal with Universal were incredibly successful. It had its own sound and its own niche in hip-hop. It wasn't East Coast or West Coast, but a Southern style of hip-hop with gritty urban undertones that was energized by Fresh's beats.

Juvenile's *400 Degreez* was released in 1998 and proved that Cash Money could be just as successful as No Limit. *400 Degreez* hit number 9 on the Billboard Top 200 chart and eventually sold more than 4 million copies in the United States. With its electronic sound combined with Juvenile's thick New Orleans accent, Kelefa Sanneh of the *New York Times* called it "a trailblazing disc full of space-age beats." The singles "Ha" and "Back that Thang Up" received radio airplay.

Juvenile's 400 Degreez (1998) *remains the best selling album ever released by Cash Money Records.*

"Back that Thang Up" stayed on the Billboard 200 chart for more than a year and the video was very popular on MTV. Juvenile followed the successful album with *Tha G-Code* in 1999, which topped Billboard's R&B/Hip-Hop chart and reached number 10 on the Billboard 200.

Other Cash Money hits came from B.G., whose *Chopper City in the Ghetto* was released in 1999. The gangsta rap album entered Billboard's Top 200 at number nine and was certified as a *platinum record*. A significant hit was "Bling Bling," featuring the Big Tymers and Hot Boys, which gave Cash Money some mainstream attention. The song popularized the term for flaunting jewelry or anything shiny and expensive. The song reached No. 2 on the Billboard Hot 100,

> ## FAST FACT
>
> The word "bling" was first used in 1999 to mean flashy jewelry indicating wealth, according to the Mirriam-Webster dictionary. Bryan "Baby" Williams said that Lil Wayne and Mannie Fresh came up with the term in the recording studio one day.

and Lil Wayne's rap on the single turned him into a star.

Lil Wayne also contributed to Cash Money's national presence with his first solo album, *Tha Block Is Hot*. Released in 1999, it showed that he had what it took to be a star. The album went double platinum, making it to number 3 on the Billboard 200 and the top of the R&B/Hip-Hop Albums charts. The title track charted on the Billboard Top 100.

Lil Wayne and B.G. also had success as members of the Hot Boys. The group's second album, *Guerilla Warfare*, released in 1999, went platinum. It topped the Billboard R&B/Hip-Hop chart and made it to number 5 on the Billboard 200. The Big Tymers contributed to the album, and also put out two albums of their own, *How U Luv That?* and *How U Lov That, Vol. 2*. Released in 1998, the albums included raps from the other Cash Money stars as well as Baby and Mannie Fresh.

CASHING IN

As Cash Money's artists and rapidly turned out records with producer Mannie Fresh, the label's venture with Universal quickly proved to

B.G. (real name Christopher Dorsey) was one of Cash Money Records's biggest stars of the 1990s.

be extremely profitable. It was not only the number of albums they were selling but the way the company operated that helped the record label earn money. The Cash Money rappers all worked on each others' albums, so they did not have to pay guest rappers to appear. Fresh could quickly turn out original beats. While rappers for larger labels might take months and spend $1 million to make an album, Cash Money could make the album for less than $50,000 and turn out a quality product in less than a week.

With all of the material its artists produced, Cash Money had numerous albums for buyers to choose from. The record label sold half a million records each month. The popularity of the label's music surprised Universal executives. "The thing just took off, and now they're selling, like, 500,000 records a month, every month, with very little overhead," said Dino Delvaille of Universal. "That amounts to a lot of money for them and for us . . . Now we're giving them a check every month that's in the millions."

Cash Money was living up to its name. In 1999, Cash Money sold 9 million albums and brought in almost $70 million. It had four of the top 20 hits on the Billboard R&B/rap album chart in November. It surpassed Master P's No Limit as the top rap producer in New Orleans, and was selling more albums than Bad Boy and Def Jam.

SUCCESSFUL ROUTINE

Part of the reason for Cash Money's success was the experience of Baby and Slim. When they signed the deal with Universal, they were not well-known in the music industry, but they had been involved in the music business for many years.

> **FAST FACT**
>
> "Ha" was written as a song that's a question. Juvenile worked with Lump, from On the Level Promotions, while he was recording the song in Nashville. He came up with the idea, and went into the studio to record it free-form style. "'I said, 'What, the whole song's gonna be a question?' Lump recalled. "And he's like, 'The whole ... song's a question.' I went to Applebees to get something to eat and came back. Mannie did the beat in about twenty minutes, and Juve just came in ... And it was a hit. You just knew it right then."

Those who thought they were dealing with someone inexperienced were in for a surprise. "The industry looked at it like we came from nowhere," Baby said. "But I was already eight years in."

Baby and Slim made sure that success did not cause their artists to lose focus. They insisted that the Cash Money crew check in at the office outside New Orleans each day. Rappers like Juvenile agreed with their policy and saw the rewards that came from it. "When you hang around here, good things happen for you," Juvenile said. "You don't come around here once a day, or make a call, you miss out on stuff. We're always working—ain't no such thing as a vacation right now."

SHARING THE WEALTH

The Cash Money artists did not forget what it was like to grow up poor. After its artists began having success, they gave away thousands of free turkeys at Thanksgiving time in the poorer neighborhoods of New Orleans. The record label would also sponsor a barbecue on a Sunday, or have people come through the projects and give away bikes.

The Cash Money crew still returned the Magnolia Projects to visit the barbershop or grocery store. "We not the kind of people that forget about where we come from," Juvenile told writer Jason Fine of *Rolling Stone.* "That's the whole thing about success—you could have all the money in the world, but if you don't have peace of mind, and if you're not enjoying your life, then what you got it for? You only got one chance to live. My people—where I come from—all my people are struggling, and I'm, like, the only one from back there that's a major success. So I . . . try to do what's right for my people and myself."

Cash Money artists needed to be ready to record at any time, and were part of tight-knit group. In addition to the four rappers, a staff of 20 to 40 worked at the office with Slim and Baby. Cash Money did not allow friends of the artists to come to the studio, as it did not want outsiders there.

The label also had a policy that its artists should not use drugs. However, some of the rappers still battled personal problems. B.G. and Turk struggled with drug addiction. Slim and Baby tried to keep the Cash Money crew out of trouble. Cash Money wanted no part of incidents such as the ones that had gotten rappers Tupac Shakur and the Notorious B.I.G. killed and Jay-Z and Puff Daddy arrested. "When you're at the clubs or these parties you have no control over what happens," Slim said. "Then trouble starts and it's all on you. You go to jail, your career is over-and we're not having that."

LITTLE RESPECT, BUT LOTS OF CASH

Despite the record label's financial success, Cash Money was still not as well known nationally as Bad Boy and Def Jam. It received little respect from others in the the music industry. Despite the high number of albums the label was selling, none of Cash Money's releases were nominated for Grammy Awards. The label received only one American Music Award nomination. Cash Money was thought of as a music industry outsider. The label's artists didn't let the slight bother them. "I can't worry about what people think," Juvenile said. "It would be nice to get the respect we deserve, but what can you do? The work should speak for itself."

What the Cash Money artists lacked in awards they made up for with cash. They did not hide their wealth. The label flaunted its success by giving several of its rappers Bentleys. The expensive cars were customized with DVD screens on the interior, upgraded sound systems, and 20-inch custom rims. When they went on an arena tour with the Ruff Ryders, the label's artists called themselves the Cash Money Millionaires. When Juvenile performed, he jumped out of giant prop made to look like a Plexiglass Rolex.

The Cash Money rappers moved out of the poor neighborhoods where they had grown up and bought homes in upscale communities. They had the means to live a better life, and took advantage of that. "From the way we grew up, we wanted to see the other side of life, the side we watched on *The Young and the Restless* and stuff like that," Young Turk said. "We saw them livin' well, and we was livin' in the ghetto. So now we're able to live in private communities, why not?"

Times were good for Cash Money. Baby and Slim were running a profitable business and the Cash Money rappers had quickly achieved success. However, whether the label would be able to hold on to that success was another question.

stars depart

Cash Money was selling millions of albums, but trouble arose when the artists who made those albums became dissatisfied. Cash Money was bringing in profits, but Juvenile, B.G., Turk, and Mannie Fresh were not happy with the way they were being treated by the label. They felt they should be getting a larger share of the money that was coming in.

The rumblings began when Juvenile came to believe, after his 1999 tour with Ruff Ryders, that Cash Money was not paying him fairly. "I was paying attention," Juvenile told music channel VH1. "I saw stuff happening to me. Situations like you realizing that 'Yo, this paperwork was never right!'" He continued to work with Cash Money for a time, completing the album *Project English* in 2001. He left the label the next year, however, saying that he could no longer trust Cash Money to treat him fairly.

B.G. released *Checkmate* in 2000, which was certified as a **gold record**, but he too began to question the amount he was being paid. He soon decided to leave Cash Money and form his own label, Chopper City Records. B.G. later said that he believed Cash Money had taken advantage of his youth when they signed him to a recording contract. "I was young," B.G told MTV News. "I didn't know no better. I looked up to them and respected them. I felt like they wouldn't do me like that, but I was wrong."

Turk followed a similar pattern. After Cash Money released his album *Young and Thuggin'* in 2001, Turk left the label for Koch Records.

The Williams brothers were upset when rappers began to leave their label. They had worked with these rappers for many years and helped them go from obscurity to success. Baby told *Vibe* magazine that Cash Money Records was so important to him that he felt abandoned when the rappers left. "That really opened my eyes," he said.

> ## FAST FACT
>
> After Turk left Cash Money for Koch Records in 2001, he had troubles in his personal life. In 2004, he was convicted of second-degree attempted murder for shooting a police officer. Turk was sentenced to 12 years in prison.

PLUGGING AWAY

Despite the problems with its artists, Cash Money continued to turn out albums, although not all reached the levels of success of its previous efforts. Lil Wayne's *Lights Out* (2000) and *500 Degreez* (2002) reached gold, but not platinum, status.

With the loss of so many of his young stars, Baby put more effort into his own rapping career. He and Mannie Fresh had more success as the Big Tymers. Their album *I Got That Work* went platinum in 2000 and *Hood Rich* (2002) reached the top of the Billboard Hot 200, the first Cash Money album to take the top spot. The single "Still Fly" made it to number 11 on the Billboard Hot 100 and was nominated for a Grammy for Best Rap Performance by a Duo or Group in 2003. The Big Tymers also released *Big Money Heavyweight* in 2003, although it was not as successful.

Baby and Mannie Fresh ventured into solo careers as well. Mannie released *The Mind of Mannie Fresh* in 2004, and Baby rapped under the name Birdman on his solo albums. Fresh and Lil Wayne were featured on several tracks of *Birdman*, released in 2002. They were also featured on Birdman's 2005 release, *Fast Money*, an album he enjoyed making because it gave him the opportunity to spend time in New Orleans and brought him back to the his roots. "We were traveling so much, all over the place. This is the first time that I've settled myself down and was able to record without being on the road," he said. "You're going to feel that Cash Money vibe—that music that everybody loved that we came into the game with. All I wanted to do was bring back that feeling."

Cash Money also experimented with bringing in a new sound to the label. Mack 10, a West Coast rapper who had been working with Priority Records, signed with Cash Money in 2001 and

Performing under the name Big Tymers, Bryan "Baby" Williams
(left) and Mannie Fresh had several hits for Cash Money Records.
Both also released solo albums for the label in the early 2000s.

released *Bang or Ball* later that year. The album made it to number 4 on Billboard's R&B/Hip-Hop albums chart. Although the album was criticized for having too much of the same sound, *All Music Guide* reviewer Jason Birchmeier, gave Cash Money and Mack 10 credit for taking a chance at bringing West Coast and Southern rap together. "By the time you hit the halfway mark, the album begins to sound a big monotonous," he said. "Still, *Bang or Ball* is an engaging listen, especially the first time through."

The label also received help from its former stars. Baby admitted that mistakes were made with the way he treated his young stars. "All of them took me to court and I paid the price for it," he told *Billboard* magazine. The label reached an agreement with Juvenile after Juvenile sued the record label, and Cash Money released *Juve the Great* in 2003. The single "Slow Motion," featuring Soulja Slim, reached No. 1 on the Billboard Hot 100. Juvenile was also part of one more Hot Boys release, *Let 'Em Burn* (2003), but did not return to the label.

West Coast rapper Mack 10 had released three successful albums for Priority Records before moving to Cash Money Records in 2001. He would release one Cash Money album, Bang or Ball, *which was a modest hit for the label.*

TEENA MARIE

California-born singer Teena Marie is a white R&B singer with soul. She signed with Motown Records in 1976 and released her first album in 1979. It was produced by her friend Rick James, a popular R&B and funk singer. Her hits include a duet with James, "Fire and Desire." Other hits for Teena Marie include "Behind the Groove," "Lover Girl," "I Need Your Lovin,'" and Square Biz.

"I've always been accepted by the black community and I think that's a beautiful thing," she told *Jet* magazine. "I wanted to sing R&B. I've just been doing music that I like to do."I think that makes me, me," she added. "It's from my heart."

Teena Marie released two albums with Cash Money Records, *La Doña* in 2004 and *Sapphire* in 2006. However, in 2009 she moved to the Stax label for the release of *Congo Square*.

In December 2010, Teena Marie died at the age of 54.

Despite its financial missteps and legal troubles, Cash Money endured. While Baby kept things going musically at the label, Slim kept working the business side of the organization. "We've got one shot. That's how I look at things," Slim told *Billboard*. "This is a job, not a party. I see Cash Money as a big movie. As long as we stick to the script and don't jump out of character, we'll be fine."

NEW DIRECTION

Cash Money did not veer from its dedication to making music. However, as artists left the label, it did change the type of music it produced. In 2004, the label signed R&B singer Teena Marie. When the deal was first made, some wondered if Cash Money knew what it was doing. Slim was certain that the label was on the right track, however. Any questions people had about the wisdom of the deal only made him work harder.

Expanding into other musical realms was not unheard of in the world of hip-hop record labels. For example, Def Jam had established a Def Soul Classics imprint that featured the work of soul singers. However, Cash Money's move to sign Teena Marie was a surprise to executives at Universal, which marketed Cash Money's music. "You don't expect a hip-hop label to sign an R&B artist," said Michael Horton, the senior vice president of promotion at Universal. "But at the same time, it was brilliant."

Cash Money created a new label for its R&B Acts, called Roun'Table Entertainment to help the label diversify beyond rap. To survive, the company

FAST FACT

In 2004, Lil Wayne made the first of many guest appearances of his career, rapping on "Soldier" for Destiny's Child.

needed to expand. "It's important for any label to diversify and open up its roster to other genres," said Merlin Bobb, CEO of Roun'Table. "It makes sense for growth."

The label's work with new musical styles paid off. Mannie Fresh helped Teena Marie produce the album *La Doña*, which made it to number six on the on the Billboard 200 and number three on the R&B/Hip-Hop chart. The single "Still in Love" received national radio airplay.

SUCCESS AND A SHOCK

Cash Money continued to have success with rap as well. In 2005 Lil Wayne's fourth album, *Tha Carter*, was released in 2004 and reached No. 5 on the Billboard 200, his best showing as a solo artist. "Go DJ" was a hit single, and Fresh continued to deliver an effective beat.

Cash Money received a surprise in 2005, however, when Fresh announced he was leaving the label. Fresh was a talented producer who had created Cash Money's signature sound. However, Fresh felt that he was not being treated fairly by the label and was not being paid what he was worth. He left the label to look for work elsewhere.

Not long after Fresh left, Cash Money was dealt another blow. Hurricane Katrina pummeled the Gulf Coast in August 2005. The city of New Orleans flooded after the storm surge overwhelmed the levees that were supposed to hold the water back. Baby and Lil Wayne had their homes destroyed. The Cash Money offices were flooded. Cash Money would have to rebound, and rebuild, from a new headquarters.

Flooded homes in New Orleans with the city skyline in the background, September 2005. Hurricane Katrina caused an estimated $81 billion in property damage and led to the deaths of more than 1,800 people.

5

lil wayne takes off

ash Money relocated to Miami and set about rebuilding its business. Without Mannie Fresh to produce the label's albums, Cash Money faced the challenge of finding new producers who could create interesting beats. While this was a challenge, it also gave the label an opportunity to change the way it did things. "I think [Mannie's departure] was a gift and a curse," said Baby. "The curse is 'cause I never would have wanted [his leaving] to be like that, 'cause I came up with him. But [the change] gave us an opportunity to start molding our talent. Now we get to pick what we like and what we think people like."

Because of the devastation caused by Hurricane Katrina, the Williams brothers moved the headquartes for Cash Money Records to Miami.

Moving forward without Mannie Fresh would not be easy, but the Williams brothers were still hungry for success. They had worked hard to build Cash Money and did not consider letting the label go.

LIL WAYNE FOR PRESIDENT

The departure of Fresh and the other Hot Boys left Lil Wayne as the only Cash Money artist left in the fold. He briefly considered leaving the label as well. Well-known New York rapper Jay-Z had invited Lil Wayne to join his Roc-A-Fella Records. In fact, at a concert in New York Lil Wayne told the crowd he would be moving to Roc-A-Fella. However, Lil Wayne's strong ties to Baby made it difficult for him to depart.

Ultimately, Lil Wayne decided he could not leave Cash Money. He later said his comments about Rock-A-Fella were blown out of propor-

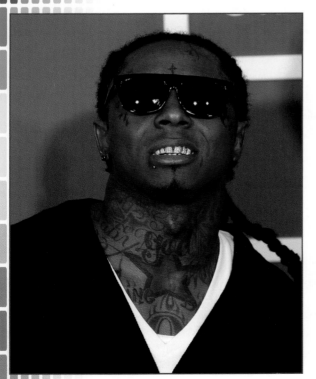

tion. He was simply looking for a home for his own music label, Young Money Entertainment, which he had founded in 2003. The Williams brothers offered

In 2007, Lil Wayne (pictured) signed the first artists to his Young Money label, Mack Maine and Gudda Gudda. Both had known Wayne since they were children.

to help distribute Young Money releases, and also offered Lil Wayne the position of president of Cash Money Records.

As president, Lil Wayne would have full creative control over all releases under the two labels. However, he did not hold the position for long. In 2007, Lil Wayne resigned from the leadership position, saying that he wanted to concentrate on his music.

PLENTY OF MATERIAL

Between 2005 and 2008, Lil Wayne's world included almost nonstop recording. At the end of 2005 he released *Tha Carter II*, his first album without producer Mannie Fresh. On the album, which used the skills of a number of producers, he called himself the best rapper alive and cut down radio stations that hesitated to play Southern rap. In his song "Shooter," he rapped:

> And to the radio stations, I'm tired o' being patient
>   Stop bein' rapper racists, region haters
> Spectators, dictators . . .
>   But this is Southern face it
> If we too simple then y'all don't get the basics

Someone was listening, as the album sold more than 1.8 million copies. It topped Billboard's R&B/Hip-Hop chart and made it to No. 2 on the Billboard 200. His pointed style made an impression on *New York Times* writer Kelefa Sanneh. "He sounded like a rapper with something to prove," she said. "Lil Wayne worked overtime, using his croaky voice to deliver sharply written rhymes."

Lil Wayne had a seemingly unlimited number of rhymes to deliver. Instead of releasing another album, he reached out to fans with mixtapes. The mixtape *Dedication 2*, which he recorded with DJ

Drama in 2006, included a song criticizing President George W. Bush for the government's response to Hurricane Katrina. Another mixtape, *Da Drought 3*, was released in 2007 as a free download. In addition, during this time Lil Wayne made many appearances on other artists' songs. These included Fat Joe's "Make it Rain," Chris Brown's "Gimme That," and Lloyd's "You."

In 2006, Lil Wayne **collaborated** with Bryan Williams (who again recorded as Birdman) on the Cash Money album *Like Father, Like Son.*

> ===**FAST FACT**===
>
> The name of the 2006 album by Lil Wayne and Birdman (Bryan "Baby" Williams), *Like Father, Like Son*, was appropriate. For many years, Williams had been like a father to Lil Wayne, whose stepfather had been killed when Wayne was a teenager. Williams was the one who picked Wayne up from school and took care of him afterward. "I was schooling the young 'un since he was 11," Baby later explained. "He stayed at my house. I took him to school. I did everything a daddy did."

Songs on the album were about money and crime. They included "Stuntin' Like My Daddy" and "Out to the Pound." The *New York Times* called their effort "an affable and mainly excellent collaboration."

Baby and other Cash Money artists continued to release albums. Teena Marie's *Saphire* came out in 2006, and Birdman released *5 * Stunna* the next year. Two volumes of *10 Years of Bling* were released in 2007 and 2008. The albums were credited to Cash Money Millionaires, a collection of rappers signed to the Cash Money label. However, Lil Wayne clearly remained the label's star.

POPULARITY AND PROBLEMS

Lil Wayne's popularity and reputation reached new levels in 2008

Lil Wayne and Birdman pose for a photo to promote their 2006 album Like Father, Like Son.

*Music producer and rapper DJ Khaled was one of several performers who appeared on "100 Million," the second single from Birdman's 5 * Stunna album.*

with the release of *Tha Carter III*. The album went platinum in one week and sold almost 3 million copies. The singles "Lollipop," "A Milli," and "Got Money" were all in the top 10 in the same week on the Hot Rap Songs chart, and "Lollipop" topped the Billboard Hot 100. *Tha Carter III* was nominated for eight Grammy Awards in 2009, with Lil Wayne winning awards for Album of the Year, Best Rap Song ("Lollipop"), and Best Rap Solo Performance ("A Milli"). In addition, Lil Wayne won a BET award as Best Male Hip-Hop Artist.

After the release of *Tha Carter III*, Lil Wayne embarked on a concert tour that brought in more money than any previous rap tour, according to the industry magazine *Billboard Boxscore*. In 2008 and 2009, his "I Am Music" and "America's Most Wanted" arena and amphitheater tours brought in $39 million in North America. Between December 2008 and September 2009, he performed 68 shows for more than 700,000 fans. "You have to perform every night and you have to execute every night," Lil Wayne said. "You build it and they will come."

LEGAL TROUBLES

Lil Wayne was a talented rapper who could deliver seemingly effort-less rhymes. With the success of *Tha Carter III*, both Lil Wayne and Cash Money Records were thriving. However, the label's star was not without his problems. He was bold and brash, and his personality could be abrasive. He was sued by people who claimed they had not been paid for their work on *Tha Carter III*. Concerns about Lil Wayne's drug use and party lifestyle also drugs cast a shadow over his bright career. *Vibe* magazine called the rapper "a slightly unhinged live wire with a taste for the dramatic and a boastful conviction that everything he does, or wants to do, is justified simply because of who he is."

There was no doubt that he worked hard. Lil Wayne continued to record at a feverish pace, making guest appearances on other artists' songs and making his own mixtapes. For all that he had accom-plished, he said that he still felt he had more to do. "I still feel like I'm not being respected," he told *Vibe*. "That's the scary part. I still feel like I don't have the crown. I still feel there's something I have to do that hasn't been done."

Lil Wayne once said that in a recording studio, he felt like he was in a classroom where he knew all the answers. Outside of the studio, however, the rapper got into serious trouble. In 2007, after a perform-ance, he was arrested in New York City and charged with criminal pos-session of a weapon and marijuana. In October 2009, he went to trial, pled guilty, and was sentenced to serve a year in prison.

Before starting to serve his sentence in March 2010, Wayne worked at a frantic pace. In a studio on his tour bus, he recorded three albums and a mixtape. A documentary about film about him

Police officers escort Lil Wayne to New York's Rikers Island prison facility, March 2010. Although he was sentenced to a year in prison, the rapper was released after eight months because of his good behavior while in jail.

and his work, *Tha Carter*, was released in November 2009. It showed his obsession with recording. After Lil Wayne was sentenced to jail, Baby told him to continue making the music that he loved in order to get through the difficult times. "That's the only thing we've got," Baby said. "Music, that's the only thing that gets the stress off your mind to make you feel better."

Nicki Minaj's debut album Pink Friday, released by Lil Wayne's Young Money and Cash Money Records in 2009, was a huge hit. The album hit number one on the Billboard chart and sold 1.5 million copies.

New Stars Emerge

ash Money Records has never relied on one star for its success. This helped the label continue to do well after Lil Wayne went to prison. Its artists also allowed the label to go in a number of different directions.

Kevin Rudolf gave the label a new sound with the release of *In the City*, and the popular single "Let it Rock," in 2008. The first female rapper to have significant success on the Cash Money label was Nicki Minaj, who charted with "Your Love" in 2010. Drake, an actor turned rapper, had a 2009 hit with the single "Best I Ever Had." He was also part of the successful Every Girl with Young Money Entertainment group, which also included Jae Millz, Gudda Gudda, Mack Maine, and Lil Wayne. The group had a hit in 2010 with "BedRock."

Jay Sean was another successful Cash Money artist who helped the label diversify. His up-tempo tunes had a much softer sound than the gangsta-style rap of the label's early years. It was a rapper who noticed the performer, however, and brought him to Cash Money. Lil Wayne brought Jay Sean to the label after seeing him on YouTube. Sean, who had been dropped by his former record label after his first album,

DRAKE

Before he became a popular music performer, Drake was familiar to fans of the television show *Degrassi: The Next Generation* as Jimmy Brooks. On the popular series he played a basket-ball star who was shot during a school shooting and becomes disabled.

Aubry Drake Graham, a native of Toronto, began his career as a rapper and singer when he released the mixtape *Room for Improvement* in 2006. The next year he released the *Comeback Season* mixtape, which included the popular track "Replacement Girl." In 2009 he signed with Lil Wayne's Young Money label, which released Drake's mixtape *So Far Gone* (2009) and album *Thank Me Later* (2010) in collaboration with Cash Money Records.

Recognition came quickly to the singer. He was nominated for a Grammy for Best Rap Solo Performance for his 2009 single "Best I Ever Had." The song reached the top of the R&B/Hip-Hop chart and No. 2 on Billboard's Hot 100.

Drake collaborated with a number of top rap stars, including Eminem, Lil Wayne, Kanye West, and Trey Songz. His second album for Young Money/Cash Money, *Take Care*, was released in the fall of 2011.

Jay Sean's first single for *Cash Money Records*, was a number one hit in the United States in 2009. The British rapper is of Indian and Punjabi descent.

In 2010, producers Marcello "Cool" Valenzano and Andre "Dre" Lyon joined the Cash Money Records team. Cool & Dre are the label's first in-house producers since Mannie Fresh left in 2005.

quickly had a hit for Cash Money. His debut single for the label, "Down," was a collaboration with Lil Wayne that made it to the top of the Billboard Hot 100 in 2009.

MISSTEPS

While the new Cash Money artists were enjoying popularity with their releases, Baby and Lil Wayne hit a bump in the road with their albums. Baby released *Priceless* in 2009, but the album received bad reviews. *Rolling Stone* noted that "Lil Wayne's mentor has more money than rhymes," and added, "The title track finds Timbaland delivering a subpar beat, and the cameos by Wayne can't save *Priceless* from feeling ho-hum."

> **= FAST FACT =**
>
> B.G. continued to record after leaving Cash Money, but also ran into trouble with the law. He released *Too Hood 2 Be Hollywood* in 2009 and *Hollyhood* in 2010. However, B.G. was arrested in New Orleans in 2009 on a weapons charge.

Lil Wayne tried something new with his next album, *Rebirth*—he ventured into rock. However, the music was not well received. "Wayne's rock debut, 'Rebirth,' is a thoroughly misguided, all-over-the-place dud that deserves all the sneers, jeers and laughs it will undoubtably receive," said reviewer Patrick Ferrucci, who added that he hoped Lil Wayne would return to rap music.

In addition to these mediocre reviews, Cash Money also continued to have its share of legal problems. Some artists it had worked with in the past claimed they had not been paid for their work. The producer Sondrae "Bangladesh" Crawford sued Lil Wayne for *royalties* for work he had done on *Tha Carter III*. Jim Josnin sued for missed

Kevin Rudolf scored a top-ten hit for Cash Money with the single "Let it Rock," which featured a rap by Lil Wayne. The single "I Made It" from his second album, To the Sky, *featured other Cash Money artists Lil Wayne, Birdman, and Jay Sean.*

royalty payments from "Lollipop," and Play-N-Skillz said it had not received money for "Got Money," featuring T-Pain and Lil Wayne.

ENDURING SUCCESS

Despite a few subpar releases and some legal issues, Cash Money endured. Other rap labels had risen and fallen in the 20-plus years that Cash Money had been involved in the music industry, but the label expanded and grew. The Williams brothers credited the label's continued success to its ability to stay focused, make good decisions, and record the work of great artists. Cash Money was attractive to new artists, they said, because it gave them control over their music. It continued to produce popular music because it stayed in touch with the sounds that people wanted to hear.

Cash Money also survived by working with a diverse group of artists and maintaining control over the way it did business. It could make quick decisions and act on them. "If I was making moves the way corporate wanted us to make moves, I probably wouldn't be in business, because they really don't know how to hustle how we hustle," Baby said.

The label's star, Lil Wayne, was a hard worker who was not about to let a pause in his career put a stop to his music. Even though he was in jail, Lil Wayne continued to make an impact on the music scene. He had recorded so much material before he went in that there was plenty to release while he was away from the recording studio. An extended play CD *I Am Not A Human Being* was released in September 2010. *Tha Carter IV* was released later that year, to coincide with Wayne's release from prison.

For all of its success, Baby felt that Cash Money had much more to offer. He had his eyes set on being a billionaire, but it wasn't all about money and fame. Baby said he would keep working because he was driven to be the best, telling the *Miami New Times*. "I want to do more in the business than anyone ever did."

Chronology

1991   Ronald "Slim" Williams and Bryan "Baby" Williams found Cash Money Records.

1992   Cash Money releases its first album, *Sleepwalker* by Kilo-G.

1994   U.N.L.V releases *Straight Outta Tha Gutta.*

1995   Baby and Slim decide to get rid of all Cash Money artists except B.G.; Lil Wayne joins Cash Money at age 11; Lil Wayne and B.G., performing as the B.G.'s, release *True Story.*

1996   B.G. releases *Chopper City*, which has more of a gangsta feel than previous Cash Money releases.

1997   Four Cash Money artists, Juvenile, B.G., Lil Wayne, and Turk, form the Hot Boys and release *Get It How U Live!* The artists also rap on each other's solo albums. Juvenile releases *Solja Rags*, which is ranked on *Billboard*'s R&B/Hip-Hop chart, and B.G. releases *It's All On U Vol. 1* and *Vol. 2.*

1998   Cash Money signs a distribution deal with Universal worth $30 million; Baby and Mannie Fresh form the Big Tymers and release *How U Luv That? Vol 1* and *Vol. 2*; Juveniles's *400 Degreez* reaches number 9 on the Billboard Top 200 chart. It sells more than 4 million copies, becoming the best-selling album in Cash Money history.

1999   Cash Money's releases include B.G.'s *Chopper City in the Ghetto, Guerilla Warfare* by the Hot Boys, *Tha Block is Hot* by Lil Wayne, and Juvenile's *Tha G-Code.* The term "bling" is popularized by a song on

Chronology

the *Chopper City* album; the label sells 9 million albums and brings in $70 million.

2000 Cash Money releases the video and album *Baller Blockin*. The Big Tymers release *I Got That Work*, while B.G. puts out *Checkmate*. Lil Wayne releases his second solo album, *Lights Out*. Cash Money's young stars begin to question how they've been treated by the label. B.G. leaves over financial differences.

2001 West Coast rapper Mack 10 signs with Cash Money and releases *Bang or Ball*; Turk releases *Young & Thuggin*, but then leaves Cash Money. Juvenile does the same after *Project English* comes out.

2002 Bryan "Baby" Williams, rapping as Birdman, releases the solo album *Birdman*. With Mannie Fresh, Baby also releases *Hood Rich* by the Big Tymers. Lil Wayne's *500 Degreez* is not well received.

2003 The Big Tymers release *Big Money Heavyweight*. Juvenile sues Cash Money and settles out of court. *Juve the Great* is released.

2004 Cash Money moves in a new direction by signing rhythm and blues singer Teena Marie. She releases *La Doña* on the label. Lil Wayne releases *Tha Carter*. Mannie Fresh puts out a solo album, *The Mind of Mannie Fresh*.

2005 Producer Mannie Fresh leaves the label. Baby raps as Birdman on *Fast Money*, and Lil Wayne releases *Tha Carter II*, his first album without Mannie Fresh. Lil Wayne's Young Money Entertainment becomes part of Cash Money Records, and Lil Wayne becomes president of Cash Money Records.

Chronology

2006 Birdman and Lil Wayne collaborate on *Like Father, Like Son*. Teena Marie releases her second and final album for Cash Money, *Sapphire*.

2007 Birdman releases *5 * Stunna*. Lil Wayne gives up his leadership roles with Cash Money and Young Money Entertainment to focus on his rapping career.

2008 Lil Wayne's *Tha Carter III* goes platinum in one week and sells almost 3 million copies. Its singles "Lollipop," "A Milli," and "Got Money" all hit the top ten in the same week. Cash Money moves in a new direction with Kevin Rudolf, whose single "Let It Rock" is a major hit.

2009 Jay Sean and Lil Wayne have a hit with the single "Down." Sean releases the album *All or Nothing*. Young Money Entertainment artists Lil Wayne, Drake, Jae Milz, Gudda Gudda, Micki Minaj, Tyga, and Lloyd release the album *We Are Young Money* and have a hit with the single "Bedrock." Birdman puts out the album *Priceless*, and Drake releases the extended play album *So Far Gone*. Lil Wayne is sentenced to a year in prison for illegally possessing a weapon.

2010 Lil Wayne ventures unsuccessfully into rock with his album *Rebirth*. Drake releases *Thank Me Later*, while Kevin Rudolf puts out his second album, *To the Sky*. Producers Cool & Dre join the label.

2011 Cash Money Records artist Nicki Minaj wins the BET Best Female Hip Hop Artist award.

2012 Rock band Limp Bizkit signs with Cash Money Records in February.

GLOSSARY

bounce—a style of rap music with roots in New Orleans that is based on the "drag rap" beat.

collaborate—to work with others on a project.

distributor—a company that works with a record label to get music albums into retail stores and outlets where they can be sold.

gangsta rap—a style of rap music that emphasizes violence, drug use, and hostility toward women and authority as it describes inner-city life.

gold record—a record that sells at least 500,000 copies.

platinum record—a record that sells a million copies.

rapper—a performer who uses a rhythmic spoken word style.

record label—a company that produces, promotes, and distributes recordings for their artists.

rhythm and blues—a style of music, often called R&B, with a strong beat and simple chords. It has its roots in blues and African-American folk music.

royalties—payments made to a writer, composer, or contributor based upon how many copies of the work are sold.

sample—to take short snippets of another performer's song and use them in a different way in a new recording.

synthesizer—an electronic musical keyboard instrument that produces a distinctive and unusual sound.

Further Reading

Mickey Hess, ed. *Icons of Hip Hop: An Encyclopedia of the Movement, Music, and Culture.* Westport, Conn: Greenwood Press, 2007.

Norris, Chris. "Lil Wayne Goes to Jail," *Rolling Stone* (February 18, 2010), p. 42.

Ogbar, Jeffrey O.G. *Hip-Hop Revolution: The Culture and Politics of Rap.* Lawrence: University of Kansas Press, 2007.

Torres, John Albert. *Lil Wayne.* Hockesin, Del.: Mitchell Lane Publishers, 2010.

Waters, Rosa. *Hip-Hop: A Short History.* Philadelphia: Mason Crest Publishers, 2008.

White, Trey. *The Story of Death Row Records.* Philadelphia: Mason Crest Publishers, 2012.

Internet Resources

http://www.cashmoney-records.com

The official website of Cash Money Records includes information about the label's artists, videos, free downloads of music, concert tour schedules, and other information.

http://www.birdmanstunna.com

The music of Bryan "Baby" Williams, who raps under the name Birdman, is featured on this site. It also includes a bio of Birdman as well as photos.

http://www.neworleansonline.com/neworleans/music

Find information about the musical history of New Orleans on this site.

www.vibe.com

News about hip-hop and rap artists and information on the latest releases is available on this site.

http://www.weareyoungmoney.com

Information on the artists signed to Lil Wayne's Young Money Entertainment is available on this site. It also includes tour information and news.

Publisher's Note: The Web sites listed on this page were active at the time of publication. The publisher is not responsible for Web sites that have changed their address or discontinued operation since the date of publication. The publisher reviews and updates the Web sites each time the book is reprinted.

index

Entries in **bold italic** refer to captions

TERRI DOUGHERTY is a writer from Appleton, Wisconsin, who has written more than 80 books. She enjoys soccer, skiing, and music.